Oregon

by the Capstone Press
Geography Department

Reading Consultant:
Carole Gutierrez
Vice President
Portland Chamber of Commerce

CAPSTONE PRESS
MANKATO, MINNESOTA

C A P S T O N E   P R E S S

818 North Willow Street • Mankato, Minnesota 56001

Copyright © 1997 Capstone Press. All rights reserved. No part of this book
may be reproduced without written permission from the publisher.

Printed in the United States of America.

Library of Congress Cataloging-in-Publication Data
    Oregon/by the Capstone Press Geography Department
    p. cm.--(One Nation)
    Includes bibliographical references (p. 46) and index.
    Summary: Gives an overview of the state of Oregon, including its
    history, geography, people, and living conditions.
    ISBN 1-56065-501-1
    1. Oregon--Juvenile literature. [1. Oregon.]
    I. Capstone Press. Geography Dept. II. Series.
F876.3.O73 1997
979.5--dc20

                                   96-35115
                                     CIP
                                       AC

Photo credits
James P. Rowan, cover
Flag Research Center, 4 (left)
Unicorn/Brenda Matthiesen, 4 (right), 5 (left)
Cheryl Richter, 5 (right), 30
Daybreak/Richard Day, 6, 8; Susan Day, 10
FPG, 25; Richard Johnston, 12; Ron Thomas, 22;
    W.G. Carroll, 28; Guy Marche, 32; James Randklev, 34
Chuck Place, 16, 21, 26
Root Resources/Larry Schaefer, 18

Table of Contents

Fast Facts about Oregon

State Flag

Location: In the northwestern United States, along the Pacific Ocean

Size: 97,060 square miles (251,418 square kilometers)

Population: 23,081,000 (1994 United States Census Bureau figures)

Capital: Salem

Date admitted to the Union: February 14, 1859; the 33rd state

Western Meadowlark

Oregon Grape

Largest cities:
Portland, Eugene,
Salem, Gresham,
Beaverton, Medford,
Corvallis,
Springfield,
Hillsboro,
Lake Oswego
Nickname: The Beaver
State
State animal:
American Beaver

State bird: Western
Meadowlark
State flower: Oregon
Grape
State tree: Douglas Fir
State song: *"Oregon,
My Oregon"* by J. A.
Buchanan and Henry
B. Murtagh

Douglas Fir

5

Chapter 1

The Columbia River Gorge

Hood River, Oregon, lies along the Columbia Gorge. A gorge is a narrow passage through steep walls of rock. The wind and waves of the Columbia Gorge are just right for sailboarding.

Sailboards are surfboards with sails. Riders stand on their boards. They pull hard at the sails. The sails catch the wind. The riders quickly turn their boards and ride the waves.

Hood River is the World Capital of Sailboarding. People from all over the world go there to sailboard.

The Columbia River Gorge is a narrow passage through steep walls of rock.

Near the Columbia River Gorge

There is much to see and do near the gorge. The Cascade Mountains stand on both sides of the Columbia River. Oregonians and visitors ski down nearby Mount Hood. They also fish in streams that empty into the river.

Many people drive along the Columbia River Scenic Highway. They can stop to see waterfalls. Multnomah Falls drops 620 feet (186 meters).

Other Outdoor Attractions

Oregonians love the outdoors. They raft through Hells Canyon. This is the nation's deepest river gorge. They take boat tours of Crater Lake. This is the nation's deepest lake.

Oregon's cities offer outdoor fun, too. Oregonians and visitors enjoy Portland's rose gardens. Portland is called the City of Roses.

Eugene is nicknamed Tracktown USA. It draws runners from all over the world. They train at the University of Oregon's track.

Oregonians try to keep their cities, forests, and water clean. That is why many people are moving to Oregon.

Multnomah Falls is along the Columbia River Scenic Highway.

Chapter 2

The Land

Oregon is a Pacific Coast state. The Pacific Ocean lies to the west. Oregon's lowest point is along the coast. Washington borders Oregon to the north. California and Nevada are to the south. Idaho is Oregon's neighbor to the east.

Oregon is also the nation's 10th largest state. Many kinds of land cover the state. Western Oregon has mountains. Between the mountains lies a rich river valley. Eastern Oregon has a large, rugged plateau. A plateau is flat land that is higher than the land around it.

Some the many beautiful landscapes in Oregon are along the Pacific Coast.

Mount Hood is in the Casades. It is Oregon's tallest point.

The Pacific Coast
Oregon's Pacific Coast is 296 miles (476 kilometers) long. Waves pound the rocky cliffs.

Fast-flowing rivers have formed bays and harbors. Coos Bay is in southern Oregon. In the north, the Columbia River meets the Pacific Ocean.

Western Mountains
The Coast Range and Klamath Mountains stand along the Pacific. The Klamath Mountains are

12

sometimes called the Siskiyou Mountains. The Cascade Mountains are farther inland.

These mountains receive more than 64 inches (163 centimeters) of rain each year. Evergreen forests grow well there. Douglas fir, spruce, and hemlock are the major types of trees.

The Coast Range stands in northwestern Oregon. This range reaches into Washington.

The Klamath Mountains are to the southwest. They stretch from Oregon into California. The Rogue River flows through the Klamaths. Rafters enjoy running the rapids of the Rogue.

The Cascades reach into Washington and California. Mount Hood is in the Cascades. This is Oregon's tallest point. It stands 11,240 feet (3,426 meters) above sea level.

The Willamette Valley

The Willamette Valley lies between the Coast and Cascade mountains. The Willamette River runs north through the valley.

This valley has Oregon's richest farmland. Fruits and vegetables grow well there. Livestock also thrives in the valley.

Eastern Oregon

The Cascade Mountains stop most rain from reaching eastern Oregon. The southeastern part of the state receives only about 10 inches (about 25 centimeters) a year. Eastern Oregon has hot summers and cold winters.

The Columbia Plateau covers most of eastern Oregon. This land has rugged, rolling hills. Much of it is irrigated for farming. Irrigate means to bring water to fields and crops. Wheat and potatoes grow well on this land. Livestock thrives there.

The Blue and Wallowa mountains are on the eastern plateau. East of the mountains flows the Snake River. It forms part of Oregon's border with Idaho. The Snake River carved Hells Canyon.

The Great Basin lies in southeastern Oregon. Mountain ridges break up flat lowlands there. Few towns or roads are in the Great Basin.

Wildlife

Seals and sea lions live along Oregon's coast. Cod and tuna are plentiful in the ocean.

Steelhead trout swim in the state's rivers. Salmon enter the Columbia River from the Pacific Ocean. They lay their eggs up river.

Bears, deer, and elk roam through the Cascades. Otter, muskrats, and beaver live in Siskiyou National Forest. Pronghorn antelope make homes in eastern Oregon.

Chapter 3

The People

Oregon is the nation's 10th fastest-growing state. Since 1990, the state has gained more than 230,000 people. Many people came from other states. They wanted Oregon's fresh air and good jobs.

Most of Oregon's early settlers lived in the Willamette Valley. More than 70 percent of Oregonians live there today.

Oregon's Largest Population Group

Almost 93 percent of Oregonians have European backgrounds. Some of them are descendants of Oregon's first white settlers.

More than 70 percent of Oregon's people live in Willamette Valley.

Migrant workers help farmers harvest crops. Migrants are people who move to do seasonal work.

Many early Oregonians came from midwestern states and Canada. Their families originally came from England, Ireland, and Scotland.

In the 1860s, immigrants arrived in Oregon. An immigrant is a person who comes to another country to settle. Immigrants came from Germany, Sweden, and Norway. In the early 1900s, Italians, Greeks, Russians, and Poles arrived.

18

The Basques came from northern Spain. Many worked on sheep ranches. Eastern Oregon still has a large Basque community.

Hispanic Americans

Hispanics make up Oregon's second-largest population group. About 4 percent of Oregonians are Hispanic. They speak Spanish or have Spanish-speaking backgrounds.

More than 75 percent of Oregon's Hispanics are from Mexico. Some are migrant workers. Migrants are people who move to do seasonal work. They help harvest Oregon's fruits and vegetables. Other Hispanics live and work in Oregon's cities.

African Americans

About 1 percent of all Oregonians are African American. A large African-American community lives in Portland.

Some African Americans came west with the early settlers. They were not allowed to buy land in Oregon, however. More African Americans moved there after the Civil War

(1861-1865). New laws gave African Americans the same rights as all Americans.

World War II brought nearly 20,000 African Americans to Oregon. Many of them worked in Oregon's shipyards.

Asian Americans

Asian Americans are Oregon's fastest-growing ethnic group. An ethnic group is a group with a common culture. More than 70,000 Asian Americans live in Oregon. Most of them came from China, Japan, Vietnam, or Korea.

Asians have come to Oregon since the late 1800s. Many Chinese worked in lumber camps and paper mills. Many Japanese became farmers.

During World War II (1939-1945), Japan was an enemy of the United States. More than 100,000 Japanese Americans were sent to prison camps. About 4,000 of them were from Oregon.

Still, the Japanese Americans were loyal. Many served in the United States Army.

Native Americans

Almost 40,000 Native Americans live in Oregon. They belong to many Indian tribes. The Warm

Many people came to work in Oregon's shipyards.

Springs, Klamath, and Umatilla are some large tribes.

Oregon has 10 Native American reservations. A reservation is land set aside for use by Native Americans. The Warm Springs Reservation is the largest reservation in Oregon. It lies east of the Cascade Mountains. Visitors can rent cone-shaped tents called tepees. They can also watch Indian dances every Sunday in the summer.

Chapter 4
Oregon History

About 15,000 years ago, people were already living in Oregon. By the 1500s, many Native American groups lived there.

The Chinook, Klamath, and Modoc were in western Oregon. The Bannock, Paiute, and Nez Perce lived in the east. The Nez Perce bred the first Appaloosa horses.

European Explorers

In the 1540s, Spanish explorers were the first non-Indians to see Oregon. But, they did not explore it.

British explorers arrived in the 1770s. Great Britain claimed the Oregon Country. This area included land from Alaska to California.

The first Spanish explorers saw Oregon's coast, but they did not explore it.

American Explorers

In 1792, Robert Gray discovered the mouth of the Columbia River. Gray named the river after his ship Columbia.

In 1805, Meriwether Lewis and William Clark arrived. They reached the Pacific Ocean from the Columbia River. The United States also claimed the Oregon Country. The United States and Great Britain agreed to occupy the Oregon Country together.

Fur Traders

Oregon was rich in beaver pelts. In 1811, traders from the Astor fur-trading company arrived. These traders built a trading post. They called it Astoria.

In 1825, a Canadian named John McLoughlin arrived. He built a trading post called Fort Vancouver. It was north of the Columbia River. This is in present-day Washington.

McLoughlin invited Americans to live south of the Columbia River. In 1834, the first Americans arrived. They settled in the Willamette Valley.

Meriwether Lewis (right) and
William Clark (left) explored
the Oregon Country for the
United States.

Thousands of pioneers began arriving in
1843. Pioneers are the first people to settle a
land. They followed the Oregon Trail. This
route started in Independence, Missouri. It
ended in Oregon City.

Statehood
In 1846, the United States and Great Britain
divided the land. The boundary was drawn
along the 49th parallel. A parallel is an

imaginary line that measures distance between the equator and the North or South pole. The United States claimed the part of the Oregon Country south of the parallel.

In 1859, the southern part of this area was admitted to the Union. Oregon became the 33rd state. Salem was the state capital. By 1860, Oregon had more than 50,000 people.

Growth and Indian Wars

Oregon continued to grow. Factories went up in Willamette Valley cities. Lumber mills buzzed throughout the state. Farming and ranching started on the Columbia Plateau.

Native Americans tried to hold on to their land. But by 1880, Oregon's Native Americans had been forced onto reservations. The Modoc, Nez Perce, and Bannock had lost their fight.

A Progressive State

In the early 1900s, Oregon passed several important laws. These laws gave Oregonians a stronger influence on their government.

Oregonians could vote on laws. They could vote on removing politicians from office. In 1912, Oregon women won the right to vote.

Salem has been the state capital since 1859.

The U. S. government hired thousands of Oregonians to build the Bonneville Dam during the Great Depression.

The Depression and World War II

The Great Depression (1929-1939) hit the whole country. Oregon's workers could not find jobs. Farmers and ranchers lost their land.

The U.S. government helped out. It hired thousands of Oregonians. They built the Bonneville Dam on the Columbia River. The dam made electric power for nearby cities and farms.

The Owyhee Dam was completed in 1932. It was built on the Owyhee River. It provided water for fields in eastern Oregon.

The United States entered World War II in 1941. Portland's shipyards built more than 1,000 ships.

Modern Oregon

Thousands of people continued to move to Oregon. New companies moved there, too. This growth polluted the Willamette River. In the 1960s, Oregon passed new laws. These laws help keep the state's rivers clean.

A 1971 law keeps litter down. Bottles and cans for beverages must be refundable, which means people can turn them in for cash.

Oregon's businesses have also changed. There are fewer jobs in lumbering. Logging was banned in some forests in the 1990s.

New jobs have opened up in tourism, however. Many Oregonians also work for computer companies.

Chapter 5

Oregon Business

Service industries employ the largest number of Oregonians. Manufacturing earns the single largest amount of money for Oregon. Farming and forestry are other important businesses.

Agriculture

Willamette Valley farmers raise vegetables and flower bulbs. Most of the country's grass seed grows there, too. So do most of the nation's hazelnuts. Oregon is also the nation's top grower of Christmas trees.

Apples and pears grow in the Hood River valley. The Dalles is a center of cherry growing.

Oregon is the nation's top grower of Christmas trees.

Forestry is an important business. Oregon leads the states in lumber production.

Hay, oats, and wheat grow well in eastern Oregon. Potatoes grow in its irrigated fields.

Beef cattle and sheep graze on eastern grasslands. Dairy cattle and chickens are raised in western Oregon.

Forestry

Douglas firs grow in the Cascades. Ponderosa pines grow in the Blue Mountains. These are Oregon's most valuable trees.

Parts of Oregon's forests are protected from cutting. Oregon still leads the states at producing lumber, however.

Manufacturing

Wood products are Oregon's leading goods. Lumber is used to build homes.

Foods rank second among Oregon's manufactured goods. Factories freeze or can Oregon's fruits and vegetables.

Many computer companies are near Portland. They make hardware and software.

Nike Inc.'s corporate headquarters is in Beaverton. Still, most of Nike's shoes are made in Asia.

Service Industries

Tourism is a leading Oregon service business. Travelers spend about $3 billion each year. Oregon's hotels, restaurants, and resorts make most of this money.

Trade is another important service business. The Port of Portland handles trade with other countries. Japanese cars come into the country at Portland. Oregon wheat and logs leave the port. Many of these goods are shipped to Asia.

Chapter 6
Seeing the Sights

Oregon has many beautiful sights. Many visitors enjoy the rugged Pacific Coast. Others hike the mountain trails. Still others visit towns founded by pioneers.

The Pacific Coast

Astoria is in Oregon's northwest corner. This was Oregon's first permanent American settlement. Nearby is the rebuilt Fort Clatsop. Lewis and Clark spent the winter of 1805-1806 at the fort.

Crater Lake in the southern Cascades is one of the most beautiful sights to see in Oregon.

Cannon Beach is south of Astoria. Haystack Rock stands there. This 235-foot-tall (70-meter-tall) rock towers over the beach.

Sea Lions Cave is midway down the coast. Visitors can watch sea lion pups at play.

Oregon Dunes National Recreation Area is nearby. Sand dunes there are 41 miles (66 kilometers) long. Some are more than 300 feet (90 meters) high. Visitors can ride dune buggies or horses there.

The Willamette Valley

Portland is in the far northern end of the Willamette Valley. This is Oregon's largest city. It sprang up on both sides of the Willamette River.

Forest Park is in Portland. It has the only old-growth forest in a U.S. city. An old-growth forest is an original forest that has not been replanted by humans.

Portland also has the world's smallest park. Mills End Park is only 24 inches (61 centimeters) across. For fun, people built it for elves one St. Patrick's Day.

Salem is south of Portland. It is the state capital. Salem is also home to Willamette University. This is the oldest college west of the Rocky Mountains.

Eugene is farther south. It is Oregon's second-largest city. It is home to the University of Oregon.

The Cascades

Mount Hood is in the northern Cascades. This mountain is a volcano. It last erupted in the 1800s.

Crater Lake lies in the southern Cascades. It formed when a volcano exploded. Visitors can drive, hike, or bicycle around the lake.

Farther south is Upper Klamath Lake. This is Oregon's largest natural lake. The town of Klamath Falls is on the lake. The Favell Museum is there. It has a large collection of Indian arrowheads.

Northeastern Oregon

The Dalles is on the Columbia River. This town has an Old West look. It has stores and homes from the 1800s.

Pendleton is to the east. The town holds a Western roundup each year. Working cowboys take part in it.

Nearby is the Umatilla Indian Reservation. There, visitors can learn about present-day Native American life.

Hells Canyon National Recreation Area is on the eastern border of Oregon. The Snake River winds through this land. Some visitors drive along the canyon's rim. Others ride mules or llamas into the canyon.

John Day Fossil Beds National Monument is south of Pendleton. Visitors can see plant and animal fossils. A fossil is the remains of an animal or plant that lived long ago. Some are estimated to be 55 million years old.

Central Oregon

Bend is located in the middle of the state. It sits on a bend of the Deschutes River. The High Desert Museum is in Bend. It shows Oregon's history. Visitors can walk through an Indian camp. They can visit an old Oregon mine, too.

West of Bend is the Deschutes National Forest. Lava Butte and Lava River Cave are

there. Lava Butte is an old volcanic cone.
Visitors can walk through tubes once filled
with lava. Lava is hot liquid from a volcano.

Malheur National Wildlife Refuge is east of
Bend. More than 250 different kinds of birds
live there. Red-tailed hawks and golden eagles
are two of them.

Oregon Time Line

1300 B.C.—The first people reach Oregon.

A.D. 1500—Klamath, Modoc, Nez Perce, and other Native American groups live in Oregon.

1542—Spanish ships sail along the Oregon coast.

1579—The English explorer Sir Francis Drake sails along the Oregon coast.

1792—Robert Gray sails into the Columbia River.

1805—Lewis and Clark reach the mouth of the Columbia River.

1811—The fur-trading post of Astoria becomes the first permanent U.S. settlement in Oregon.

1834—A missionary settlement is built in the Willamette Valley.

1843—The first settlers who traveled the Oregon Trail arrive in Oregon.

1846—Oregon becomes part of the United States.

1848—The Oregon Territory is created.

1859—Oregon becomes the 33rd state.

1883—The Union Pacific Railway reaches Portland.

1912—Oregon gives women the right to vote.

1937—The Bonneville Dam is finished on the Columbia River.

1960—Maurine Neuberger is elected as Oregon's first woman U.S. senator.

1971—Oregon becomes the first state to ban the use of nonreturnable bottles and cans.

1977—The Portland Trail Blazers win the NBA championship.

1991—Barbara Roberts becomes Oregon's first woman governor.

1990s—Oregon passes laws to protect its old-growth forests from logging.

1991—The first Nike Town store opens in Portland.

1996—Oregon holds one of the country's first ballot-by-mail elections; about 20,000 people lose their homes during floods; a wildfire burns thousands of acres of Oregon's forest.

Famous Oregonians

Beverly Cleary (1916-) Writer who created the Henry Huggins and Ramona Quimby books for children; born in McMinnville.

Abigail Duniway (1834-1915) Women's rights leader who helped women gain the right to vote in Oregon.

Matt Groening (1954-) Cartoonist whose drawings became *The Simpsons* television show; born in Portland.

Ing Hay (1862?-1952) Chinese gold-mine worker who was called Doc Hay; used herbal medicines to cure Chinese workers when they became ill.

Chief Joseph (1840?-1904) Leader of the Nez Perce Indians during the Nez Perce War of 1877; born in the Wallawa Valley.

Ken Kesey (1935-) Novelist who wrote *One Flew Over the Cuckoo's Nest* and other books; grew up in Springfield.

Jason Lee (1803-1845) Pioneer and missionary in the Willamette Valley; founded present-day Willamette University.

Phyllis McGinley (1905-1978) Writer who won the Pulitzer Prize in poetry in 1961; born in Ontario.

John McLoughlin (1784-1857) Canadian who built Fort Vancouver; known as the "Father of Oregon."

Linus Pauling (1901-1994) Chemist who won the Nobel Prize in chemistry in 1954 and the Nobel Peace Prize in 1962; born in Portland.

Ahmad Rashad (1949-) Pro football player who became a sportscaster; born in Portland.

John Reed (1887-1920) Journalist and author of *Ten Days that Shook the World*, an eye-witness account of the Russian Revolution; born in Portland.

Mary Decker Slaney (1958-) Olympic runner who set several world track records; lives and trains in Eugene.

Words to Know

fossil—the remains of an animal or plant that lived long ago

gorge—a narrow, steep-walled canyon

immigrant—a person who comes to another country to settle

irrigate—to bring water to fields and crops

lava—hot liquid that comes from a volcano

migrant worker—a person who moves to do seasonal work

old-growth—belonging to an original forest that has not been replanted by humans

parallel—an imaginary line that measures distance between the earth's equator and the South or the North pole

pelt—fur-bearing skin

plateau—flat land that is higher than the land around it

reservation—land set aside for Native Americans

tepee—a cone-shaped tent used by Native Americans on the western plains

To Learn More

Bratvold, Gretchen. *Oregon*. Hello USA.
Minneapolis: Lerner Publications, 1991.

Cleary, Beverly. *My Own Two Feet: A Memoir*. New York: Morrow Junior Books, 1995.

Cloutier, James. *This Day in Oregon*. Eugene, Ore.: Image West Press, 1981.

Fradin, Dennis Brindell and Judith Bloom Fradin. *Oregon*. Sea to Shining Sea. Chicago: Children's Press, 1995.

Riegel, Martin P. *Ghost Ports of the Pacific, Vol. II: Oregon*. San Clemente, Calif.: Riegel Publishing, 1989.

Stein, R. Conrad. *Oregon*. America the Beautiful. Chicago: Children's Press, 1989.

Useful Addresses

Columbia River Maritime Museum
1792 Marine Drive
Astoria, OR 97103

Crater Lake National Park
P.O. Box 7
Crater Lake, OR 97604

Fort Vancouver National Historic Site
612 East Reserve Street
Vancouver, OR 98661

Hells Canyon Adventure, Inc.
Box 159
Oxbow, OR 97840

High Desert Museum
59800 South Highway 97
Bend, OR 97702

Nike Town
930 SW 6th Avenue
Portland, OR 97204

Oregon Coast Aquarium
2820 Southeast Ferry Slip Road
Newport, OR 97365

Internet Sites

City.Net Oregon
http://city.net/countries/united_states/oregon

Travel.org—Oregon
http://travel.org/oregon.html

Oregon On-Line
http://www.or.gov

Experience the Columbia River Gorge
http://www.corge.com/~columbia/

Index